Giving In

Poems & Drawings
by Jessie Lian

Published by Riverwalk Press
Copyright © 2023 Jessie Lian
ISBN: 979-8-9889318-0-5

Illustrations and design by Jessie Lian
www.jessielian.com

Table Of Contents

Preface

You might ask what exactly it is I'm "giving in" to. My short answer is that, well, it's at least not giving *up*. My braver answer is that it's something still unformed, vague in shape & adolescent in age. But what I do know: it's worth giving in to. I know because it feels like falling toward gravity instead of fighting against it, like taking a deep belly breath and releasing it back, like sinking into my own skin and staying.

You could say I'm giving in to my child self, the younger me who was equal parts question mark and exclamation point. You could also say I'm giving in to my higher self, the older me who insists I try on kindness and patience and so on- especially with myself.

But then again, you could say I'm not giving into a self at all, but something invisible and sacred, with leaves and with branches, made of water and sun, releasing energy and breath. It is as much inside my lungs as it is a piece of cake. It is in the delight of a ladybug lost on my leg, in the mystery of how two people fall in love, in the pursuit of a mythical laughter, in the shadow of a tree and the terrifying thing of hope. And somehow, by giving in to it, I become a part of it, and it a part of me. Somehow, I become a winged and mythical thing in the telling of these poems. This is a puzzle I'm only beginning to piece together, and barely.

Thank you for reading what has come from this journey. I hope these poems lend a little courage to *give in* to whatever mystery invites you into life. Some days it may look like soaking in rain, other days like settling under sun. But this is our wild, unpredictable existence. Maybe we'll discover what seems to give back when we finally decide to give in.

"We have fallen into the place
where everything is music"

–Rumi

"I can't give you any advice but this: to go into yourself
and see how deep the place is from which your life flows"

–Rainer Maria Rilker

Giving In

Look Up

On my desk, the troupe of tulips have begun to droop.
      I lay on the floor and look up as they bow.
From here, they appear as if they are still rising
      as if they are on their way in and not out
and I think that perhaps I could live the rest of life like this
      like aging was the act of moving in and not out
and then like this–
          looking up–
like everything might fall toward me
      toward my pull of gravity
berries and bees dropping into my belly
      chaos dissipating in the sip of an inhale
everything getting sucked single-file into my center–
      my center– volcanic rock commanding respect–
except what is that fear that stops me mid-breath
      makes me want to repel more than revel
as if I couldn't dare dream of a life dripping with good
      as if it'd burn my center before I could burn back
Think! What sort of bright and terrifying fate
      could have such irresistible force
that it relentlessly pulls me further and further into it
      despite how I try to resist?
How is it that everything falls
      but gives to me   anyway?

WINTER

Winter is my season for wanting. The want is raw, unfiltered, even indulgent. I let myself look inward at my undressed dreams, my mean desires, my quiet darknesses. It is hunger inside hibernation, ache inside isolation, a restless sort of rest. My eyes dart back & forth beneath my eyelids. I am hesitant & hazy, waiting.

Wintering Sun

I have arranged my life to follow the movement of light. In the morning, it's a small square of sun in the center of the bed, and I sit cross-legged within it, a warm prayer. At around noon, it slips into the bathroom, dripping through a slit of window, and I run the hot water and watch the steam rise in a stream of light. It always surprises me, the way air curls around air. I indulge myself in the looking. And on some particularly special days, I'll take my lunch on the toilet lid too, spooning myself a quiet bowl of porridge and egg. Flecks of dust and other speckle and float; shadows angle and arch on the wall. The tiled floor sweats in the intimacy of this touch. Eventually, the light moves beyond this little room, leaves me shuddering and dizzy in a dream quickly dulling. I must see it one more time before it goes. When afternoon sighs into 5 p.m., I rush outside with farewells in hand, wave them in the dimming air. The gold thing sleds across asphalt, spins off the sloping earth, barely notices me. It always ends like this, imbalanced. As it ought to be. A hero slicing the sky in flight, a child staring up.

The body's young light
longs for its ancient source– to
briefly borrow bright

Pursuit Of Some Song

A wilderness rushed out of my mouth–
A type of bird, I think, or maybe a bat,
It was marked by something forgettable
It sighed a deflated hum.

I found myself running after it
Even while wondering why
I can't be sure what my aim is
Or what I'll do once it's caught

Still I'm tracking its wake of feathers
Furiously fossilizing proofs
I'm hungry to know its meaning
And why its origin was me

> *Yes why do these*
> *mundane little things*
> *buckle on wings*
> *and voluntarily fly*
> *toward a glaring*
> *scrupulous*
> *sun?*

I log every feather, classify each by word:
Gray, soft, light, thin, string them all together–
A pillowy imitation, I rummage through its center
And hope for an opening   a place for me to breathe

Breadcrumbs

Portals arrive in improbable places. Like yesterday,
it is in a bread pan, while I am making a cake,
olive oil and orange peels and then I remembered you.
Next week is- was- would've been- is- your birthday,
and we are turning fourteen in the neighborhood pool,
floating on the surface of a bubble, guzzling orange Fanta.
The wind blows out the candles in great gusty kisses.
You go with them. And leave me with only sugar and smoke,
trembling cold on the linoleum floor of my kitchen
fifteen years later. I go back to church. They are saying that
everyone is welcome at the communion table and I know that's
not what I told you. So I take the loaf whole from the altar
and chuck it to the sky, *happy birthday* I say. And the bread
breaks, and crumbles, and drops like manna back in my
lap. And there is nothing more to do, but eat.

How To Make Dumplings

Cup your hand, like you're half-cocooning
the moon's reflection, like it's glowing in a pond
at the center of your palm.

This is how upholdingly you must
let the dumpling flesh rest on yours, as you
tuck it in with cabbage and pork.

Elders around the table will cluck in disapproval,
others will chuckle and say next time, xià yī cì,
and you'll wonder if you're too American

or if this is how you'll always be seen:
a reflection of real, partial form,
baby half. My father is telling stories

in Chinglish again. About how his village
was so deserted that the dark felt almost
savory. How the moon looked like a riceball,

a promise you could just scoop out
from the bowl of the sky. And it made his mouth
water, to think back on his hunger–

how possible life looked from there.

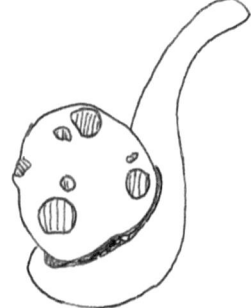

In Forty Years

After Louise Glück

What happens to the dreamers? Still
drudging up the same buttered toast
forty years. The piano box caked with dust
while someone sighs over the end
of the loaf and now

    we'll have to get more.
    It will be the cheap generic brand, as usual.
    Honey, call the neighbors when I'm away.
    Invite them to dinner, say we'll play that game we like,
    the one where we have to choose money or fame or
    a pedestrian story of love. Maybe tonight, we'll pick fame.
    Pretend like change never came. Like we're still
    dripping sweat over a blank and beckoning page and
    all its possibilities of song, song, revolutionary song and

Another revolution. Ends dipping into beginnings and still
the dazed dreams drift restless. They search for a body,
a space where a rupture is ripening within the old ritual,
a place like a table and a sleepless night, a feeling, a change,
a matchstick and bone, a marvel, a volt, a fist to oblivion.

The Faucet Is Leaking

Time is dripping from a leaking faucet
so fast I must balance a paper cup
beneath the cold-lipped spout and pray
that the seconds would be saved and
come back. *Everything, come back.*
How many friends does one lose to growing up?
I think about this while lying next to my best friend
in a second-hand bed, the last sleepover we can share
before motherhood comes and takes her. Currently, she is
heehawing about some stupid meme on her phone,
and all I want is to take her face in my hands and
slap her, tell her to resist a little, to push against
this next croaking chapter, but instead I do nothing
but bug-eyed gape, her beautiful face,
and I drink and drink, gulping this moment down
into the fish tank of my rib cage
which is swimming with days, days spilling into days,
like sardines I've packed in for days and days and
this is really no way to treat time. All frugal and scrooge.
My best friend and soon-to-be mother turns over and
looks at me. There is nothing to be done.
So I eternalize her attention in mine.
And practice the motion of closing & opening my hands–
closing as I take this single drop of honey time,
opening as I lick its sweet clean from my palms,
which are sticky with a memory, and empty,
almost ready to close again, open again,
almost ready for the next to slip through,
whatever sticky salty watery bright thing, slip through.

After Meeting You

"But it's the having not the keeping that is the treasure."
—Jack Gilbert

Make me like a sea sponge
able to let things go as easy
as I let things in- belief
that the ocean will always come back
obvious & ubiquitous like love
the stubborn insistence of love.
And suppose it never does come back.
Make me believe that it was enough
just to have momentarily tasted it, this
flood of hungry life, swimming through my pores.
How lucky, to have had it. But please
would you please still

                                        stay

Wide Wants

I want to eat the sky. I want to drink the wind.
I want to be a creaking noise, in the reaching of a tree.

I want to kiss the sun. I want to wear her hat.
I want to be a desert song, in the reflecting of her heat.

I want to dance on air. I want to drift above.
I want to be a whistling leaf, in the movement of a beat.

I want to shut my eyes. I want to sink in dream.
I want to be a resting root, in the center of earth's seat.

I want to wake up soon, go! blink in all this world,
and befriend this giant, glowing, growling sort of ache.

Flat Coincidences

When a man materializes to fix my flat tire
I almost forget to thank him, so distracted
by the near nothing probability. I consider
how he could fit into my map of coincidences,
I interrogate him for hints– but he interrupts
to ask what I'm doing at a Sam's Club
two thousand miles from home.
I explain in dominoes.
How one thing gave to the next.
Because I don't believe in coincidences
that simply dead end. Because I can't comprehend
the concept of all this life and no clear conclusion.
He looks at me funny. Later that night,
a friend and I play a game;
we pick a random number,
drive straight to that exit ramp,
simmer with shrill anticipation.
Well, we end up at a burger joint, a chain.
And order a banana milkshake, vegan.
That's it, then? Some artificial milk
in exchange for a plea of serendipity?

Ode To Acquaintances

Alone but not lonely
we say about life lately
we say about our new homes
on the other side of the country
we say *of course we miss our friends*
but mostly we're surprised
about how we miss acquaintances too–
the person you never called *but you could've*
the gift of a familiar face at a house party
the friend's roommate you never talked to
but knew. Well, this is the beginning
of our singular lives. Just one request: call me
with the infrequency of an acquaintance
and we'll re-enact that awkward thrill
of bumping into a friend's friend's friend
while buying a can of split pea soup
at the supermarket down the store.

This Solitary Pursuit

And so what, if no one else
on this groaning heave of earth
will believe
                in you?

Can they hear what your spirit wails?
Can they feel it kicking, banging on the walls in your belly,
begging you to please let it go, let it finally fly
after the thing it so wants?

Have they sat hunched over forehead to palm,
hushing it with sense, trying
to understand why it matters so much,
& what exactly *it* even is?

            An absurdity, atrocity,
what little information we're given before every leap,
what requirements of risk precede all that's worth doing.

Well, if no one else, then *you*
must be the solitary one who will still believe
                in you.

Really, what else is there left to do?
In your single jolt of breath, electric?

SPRING

If winter is for wanting, then spring is for willing. There is an urgency to the growth in spring, a feverish & forward bloom that makes me want to blush. Love makes her appearance, while longing evolves into hope. Momentum rises, rain waters, living things appear unexpectedly, and life reveals its raging resilience.

Lady Of The Spring

Who is it
that taps her cosmic cigar
all over this tray of earth

      trails behind puffs of yellow ash
      leaves the world in a lush and reveling lust

The birds, drunken and dazed
aggressively kissing & urgently singing

      The trees, shooting into neon green stilettos
      spectacling their feet & dropping their pinks–

And who is it
that prances up peduncle poles
unbuckles their petals

      pours vodka rain all over this planet's floor
      dances a spell for it all to grow, grow, grow–
                      Is it us?

Is she inside our fleshy earths too
      striking a match to our tired winters
            teasing us into that blushing, feverish life?

Crush

We're spilling night-kissed laughter
all over this cul-de-sac's gravel;
it's collecting in pools of terrified hope,
and we are sinking, the sheer everything of it.
Childish, how earnest our wishing is.
It feels like the past is trying to
muscle its way back to the present,
like these puddles are portals
to some backyard playground, five jumps
the secret code, hopscotch your way
to belonging. Slink into the hideaway,
pretend play grownups, pretend play
going on a date, batting your eyes, falling in love.
We're sinking deeper. The floor is lava ok?
If you fall you'll die you'll be nothing ok,
just a goop of laughter, swelling on the ground.

Love, A Shapeshifter

I have wasted the whole day
comparing love to loaves of bread.
I tried saying sliced, broken, staple, crust,
then versatile, variable, vessel of jam,
But love doesn't seem to want to be
like a loaf of bread

> Nor does it want to be
> the belly of a sky
> or the diving of a starling
> or the peck of a new leaf
> or a rose, or swan, or moon

> > Still my mouth cannot close, trying
> > green flood wide rush little plum
> > slow feet heavy plunge soft being–

And for a moment it purrs,
arching in the light
of my aching scrutiny

> Then, it flutters
> winged creature
> spilling shadows
> shaped like questions

Biomimicry

What do you call the state of suspension
that hangs stale between two epiphanies?
Void, abyss, depression, rest, wait, I remember
what this is, winter, ache, evidence   enough

that something still wants.
What's the word for when a dead thing
comes up for air? And to think I had thought
that my growing days were gone.

Fooled again, I mutter again,
as a bud sprouts green beneath my crusty fingernail.
Copycat, the planet scoffs, when it sees my cyclical plots.
Well, what comes next comes five feet higher - terrifying -

and then, the bloom that felt like a boom
as my color curls open, drops like little proofs
on top of what the planet already knows.
Copycat, she snickers, *Copycat!*

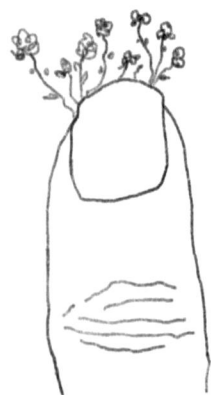

Anyone Can Plant A Potato

I learned today that you can grow
baby potatoes out of aged potatoes:
Just take a sprouting spud
And safeguard it in soil

It doesn't need you to purchase
fancy seeds packaged in pouches,
It only asks for reincarnation
and two eyes for humble observing;

I am watching it willfully grow itself,
wondering what the metaphor is:
am I more baby potato or adult potato
or both

Or is it redundant?
The root doesn't ask itself who it is–
as long as it lives, it gives, and is;
I am, then I am, so I am.

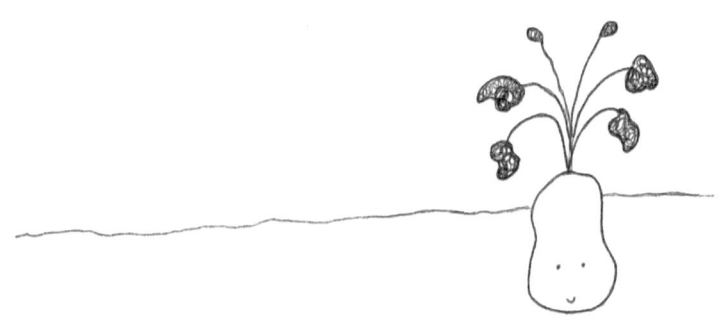

Surprises

The ant is tumbling up my leg
like a four-year-old wobbling through a ball pit.
What I mean is, sometimes you find yourself
in inexplicable places. And the ant
probably believed it had stumbled upon
some strange but delicious stump.

Meanwhile, I am fumbling across a trail of moss, oblivious
to how I've trespassed onto the hairy thumb of a mountain,
and were it not snoring through the leaves,
I'm sure it would flick me off. But today I am lucky.
Because today, I've been swept into a mountain's daydream,
and like a play, I watch the set shift, the scene change,
as impenetrable fog gives way to articulate sky,
and spider webs undress and glisten like stars,
and everything green turns silver, and I
become some misplaced extra, trying not to be found out.

What I mean is, it's never what you expect it to be,
and there'll be a mound of mud
where you expect a hill of grass,
and when you finally start the fire,
you'll be swallowed by a storm.

And you'll hide in a wooden box, that shakes within the fist
of a pound of pounding rain, like Noah's ark
and this is the daily gamble you make on living
while the whole world is set on sinking;
it is the risk we take for serendipity.

What I mean is, sometimes it's beautiful,
but sometimes I wonder if it's worth it
when the mountain awakens and shakes me off
and I fall and fall like that child and the slide and the ball pit
and the bloody knee and the squashed ant
and the slammed doors and the frozen grief
and the baby that was born on the same day as a death

And it makes me wonder what the opposite of serendipity is,
and whether it's worth it, and what to say about things that are
never what you expect them to be. There's a chance we
don't have the imagination required for accurate expectations.
But something certain is this: it will all end one day.

And it may come like relief,
or it may come like the ground beneath your house
caving in, everything crumbling.
Or it may come like the weeds & the bees, yellow and wild,
eventually finding their way onto this broken plot of land.

What I mean is, despite the surprises,
we're resilient, and when I say we're, I mean the earth,
I mean the land and the water and the sky,
I mean us as a collective, together, resilient.

And in those long moments
when we're not okay,
something somewhere
is. And have you felt it before,

when that something somewhere
invites itself into you,
right when you least expect it,
right when you think
you can't take it
a single day
more?

Q & A

The rain weathers down in great riddles,
interrogating all solid things, cement grass and sand,

and I listen to the world turned drum, turned maraca,
turned pinto beans in a cactus tube. I ask my AI

what the rain would ask the earth. Rain asks earth:
how can I best nourish and sustain you?

My body of 56% rain repeats the question half-heartedly.
The other parts, bone stuff & teeth, chew at their own center,

searching for a gravity, a tiny prophet puttering in the enamel.
I ask my AI why my sky is pink with apocalypse.

It says the sunlight is scattering– I pick it back up.
Old revelations, odd places that a sun used to make blue.

There, I find a young self preaching in a moleskine,
all capital letters. She is asking big things of me.

I try to tell her that I know even less than she does,
with questions now wide enough to hold me.

The ground caves from the memory of rain.
Holes of space I once dwelled in now

punctures of light. I ask them where
to go next, but mystery- glitches on.

Us Clouds

1.

More fragile than most days,
the sight of two birds perched on a telephone pole
is enough to make me cry.
And three days of rain was all it took to resurrect the river.
The movement is maddening,
makes me want to dance myself into foam.
My friend tells me to imagine my lungs as clouds,
air and water gathered around fire and earth.
The funny part is how quickly, even urgently, we change
from thunder to wisp. How I change shape into you.
And grow afraid of becoming so light again
that the wind would blow us back apart.
I simply mean I don't know how to hold us,
us tender ephemeral things.

2.

Today I feel stronger
bolstered by some recent good luck
and a particularly good conversation
inside the haze of a hot tub.
We kept getting in just to
get out again just to
watch ripples of steam
lift in legions from our skin.
We were microcosmic gods,
decreeing how water came and went.
I stop myself from evaporating.
And forget about the rain, move in,
toss my wet clothes on the floor.

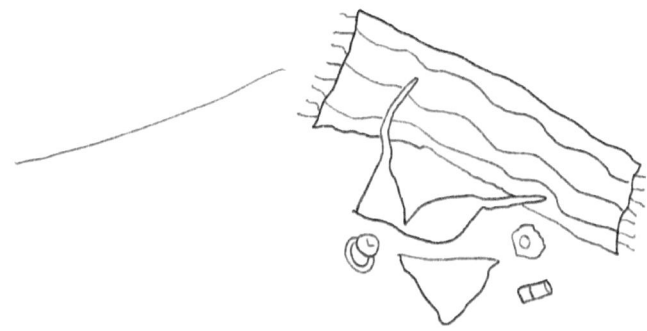

Morning After Rain

Underneath the shaking tree,
it is still raining yesterday's storm.
The tree is reliving yesterday.
And I am frozen underneath,
 reliving yesterday.

Underneath the dripping weight of
you-could'ves, you-should'ves,
I can't remember who I am.
And my fists rise like a fence
in front of my terrified face.

Later, when I realize that I'm able to simply
step out, from beneath the raining tree,
I will hang my defenses up to dry.
And I will dress myself with trust,
I will trust myself.

Yes, I will trust myself.
And that will be the only protection I need
when accusations come hailing
like little plink-plinks
of jellybeans,
ha.

Changing Seasons

Strange, how easily-
or rather, how suddenly-
a new love can find its place
in the space once reserved for another.
You had thought before that you'd
never be able to undo that body beside you
or rather, that ghost of a body beside you
until one unassuming day
like the arrival of some newly ironed house
you find yourself with a new neighbor
busily pressing out the creases
of some past sickness.
And they smell familiar
like that baggy blue shirt,
or rather, like the scent of comfort,
and you think, *good*,
how good, that love is not shy,
and will readily take the shape
of even some humble holed-up T-shirt
and eagerly hug the form
of really, any old wonder.

Tree Work

Earth's three trillion fingers
are tickling the pouting sky,
pinching her cloudy cheeks,
scooping up her pouring tears.

They are turning themselves into homes.

I long to be a drop of rain
cradled by those ancient hands,
disappearing into glowing growth,
home, in the bed of a bloom.

I am making myself, my self, a home.

Mailbox

When the day arrives for you to leave your first house,
    pluck out your mailbox.

It will make a soft sound, like a low vibrato hum.
When you wander toward the edge of the street,
away from your old outgrown walls,
your address will still stay with you,
rocking in your arms.

Walk toward the edge of the picture frame.
Wave the mailbox through the air, like a butterfly net-
catch the secrets. Like how to grow wings, and be patient;
dip it in the river like a soup ladle. Scoop up the instructions
like how to bend rocks, and move earth,
                        and be patient-

Soon, you will meet the edge.
It will only take one step, brave step, huge step
to exit the frame, into a wild Oz, where there is

hissing silence
shivering stone
spinning shadows
sitting spirits

&
a hiding song
a wiggling rock
a rocking light
a patient flame

     Here,
settle into the waves of wilderness,
welcome the arrival of strange convictions.
And each night before you sleep,
        plant your mailbox.
Unpack the envelopes, stuffed
with sidewalk, doorbell, porch, neighbor, house,
          write yourself daily

And when the letters finally arrive,
use them to build a bedroom, plant a garden, eat.
Out here, where everything is untamed, and bursts,
and everything is uncaged, and grows,
you are not far
        from home.

SUMMER

Summer is a fat pause and a giant breath. School's out; now I've got to find my own sources of fun and my own lessons to learn. I nap, heal, laugh, float. I blow bubbles, I gather sensation. My sense of presence and peace ripens as a byproduct, plumpens excellently. The sun is bright, and nothing needs to be done.

Excessive Heat Warning

All week, the heat crescendoes into the first of summer,
& I am compulsively complaining about air particles & touch.
The block has been mugged silent, a sweltering stillness,
and now is the time- to do nothing. Even the fly,
glued to the cold counter, has stopped its bothersome work.
I scrounge for the darkest place in the house. The bathroom.
Where I strip myself to skin and press my cheek against wall.
It is too hot to let anyone hold me except me,
so I cradle my body, hug my sticky knees close.
Pondering ways to disobey the sun. What I'd do,
to hold just a ray in my belly, stow the rest in the pantry,
then ration them across bad days. But instead, I am left
to figure my own light. A pathetic flicker, frequently shrouded.
Occasionally excessive. This small, unruly ball of heat.

Beneath The Shade Of A Tree

No, this isn't decadence. Go ahead
allow your fleshy spirit another hundred days
to lounge on a lawn. Concerned only with where to

lie down, where the tiny burst of a palm tree's shade
moves. Minute by minute around a trunk,
you leave a little of your shadow pooled inside the tree's.

Until you feel yourself lighter. Look, you've stopped running.
You've decided to let the memory of the thing, fear
catch up. And it's not so bad, dunking your naked

in a cold black lake, free falling in a shivering
stretch of salt. Hyperventilation, of course.
A bit of glitching and thumping. As the ghost

that once trailed like a smog long behind you
gives itself up to the gray at the foot of the plant
where moss and other miracles are making do

in that dark and restless spot of earth.

Good Art

It's past noon &
I still have not moved.
Is this depression
or meditation?
Shouldn't I be up by now,
up to something at all by now?
Wrapped up in my white blanket
I imagine I'm a popsicle stick stuck
in a glob of glue and someone
is trying to make art out of me.
Am I any good? What a needless concept.
"Good Art." I do not want to melt away
mumbling about how not-good someone's
art is. I'd rather say that at least I tried
to find the meaning the rush of art.
Ordinary & fine, art.
A popsicle stick posing,
a puddle of glue.

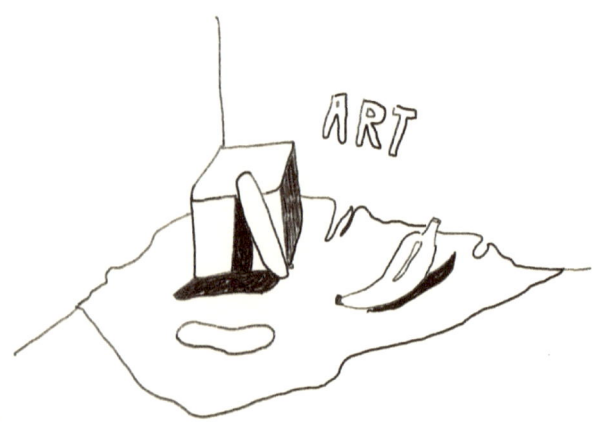

Even These Days

It would appear
that even the forgettable days-
the ones where hours stick together
mellow and monotone and bland-
even these days leave a mark on a life.
They seed into gratitude
when a day arrives different;
they eventually give rise
to a strong & upward force.
Count these days as rest, or the work of growing whole.
They let us feel our edges, glimpse out the fog of joy,
and reckon with this life, a clumsy container for a heart.
Somehow we wake up each day, and do it all again.
Somehow we shift, however small, but enough.
The miracle is the redundancy.
How we repeat ourselves endlessly
and change.

After Arriving At The Pacific

Well, I saw how small I was, so I kept going.
Drove straight into the blue 'til I was part of it.
Smudged the stiff horizon. Let saltwater into sky.
And now, there's nowhere else; we've reached our vast,

at last. Eels in trees, tentacled things freed, but I
would become a fish. Simple and scaled,
there'd be no thoughts in my tiny ocean brain,
only bug eyes and bubbles. A watery song.
The occasional ripple of desire but mostly,

nothing. It'd be enough to swim at the surface,
where the sun still touches what it likes.
Enough to arrive, anonymous, then return,
indistinguishable. A refraction of light. My eyes

two tunnels in a porous reef. Still watching,
wanting something I can't remember what.
I swim in one singular circle, then another,
a trail of bubbles, tiny explosions, there I am.
In this endless unknowable mass, there.

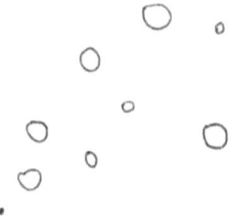

There's An Ocean Wild Inside Me

There's an ocean wild inside me
dangerous and alive and true.
It moves and moves and yet
remains unmoved.

When storms shout, and moons pull,
my ocean stomps, my ocean swings,
spills into rain, into an on and on-

My ocean is as ocean today
as it was the first day on earth.
It moves and moves and yet
remains unmoved.

And each brave day,
I wade into the creature of me
and sink.

And everywhere I dare look
when I hungry open eyes
is life- microscopic life, peeking out
from behind my bony reefs,

Gargantuan life,
singing from my belly's deep,
moving and moving and yet

remains unmoved.

The Way You Look At Your Dog

The way you look at your dog
when you say "I love you"
and grip her gaze
like a fierce unwavering plea-

that is the way you must to talk to your self:
willing the message to get on across,
with earnest urgency,
and ravenous resolve.

On The Morning Of My Birthday

I imagined myself whole,
and decided it simple:
each morning is a resurrection.
So I greet my new self with reverence.
I heat up a cup of tea on a sunbeam,
scratch the underside of a dog ear,
dig my fingers in the earth's,
sip the sky in small breaths.
I can hear the birds chirping inside me.
And I try to see where I end but I can't-

Ode To A Wild Laughter

We were sitting in a circle
cross-legged laughing
bent over laughing
foreheads pressed to the
earth laughing
until puddles of saliva
collected on the carpet
like syruped pancakes
or an archipelago
islands formed from
a family of eruptions
it felt like a little big bang
exploding in our bodies
debris and science stuff
colliding to concoct some
strange crackling
like something cracking
like the universe breaking
to make space for this
giant globe of
life so lifelike it pushes
fictional, mythical, this
is what laughter feels like
entire elephants
escaping whole from our mouths
first a trunk
appearing like a tongue
then a giant eyeball
then a big floppy ear

then an unstoppable stampede
of wrinkly legs
then earthquaking laughter
because now there would be
no, now there is
an elephant in the room
and it nearly kills us with delight
it takes up so much space
we wonder if we should
tie it down, cover it up
joy so gigantic
and embarrassingly large
so oversized
for these tiny rooms
but someone suggests
we set it free
so we do
and I cannot tell you the specifics
of what it looked like
but I like to imagine
the thing now in a field
(everything good is always in a field)
eating tree bark with the others
none of whom understand their origin
but are quite pleased with all their Wild
the point is
I'm obsessed now
with the mystery of
elephant-sized laughter
and how it is birthed
and then set free

how it can first
live in bellies and lungs
and then appear
one day like magic
in front of a clapping crowd
or alone
when you are by yourself
doing nothing but watching
the world in its funny hat
passing by the window
some Tuesday afternoon.

Roller Coaster

I let the summer sky pluck me up & dangle me high, its finger clouds. Its promise of thrill. It tickles a primal something, it makes me want life after almost death, it makes me want to be free & known before I go. I owe my confessions to no one but when I plummet to the ground they are completely unstrung & I scream them into the chest of the wind:

(

)

& I let myself be saved. Let the cracking earth catch me. Unravel into compulsive giggles, dizzy eating the ends off a fry of time, embracing all that is eternally sticky. I let myself into my own secrets, make peace. & It makes me wonder. What other dangers are only facades

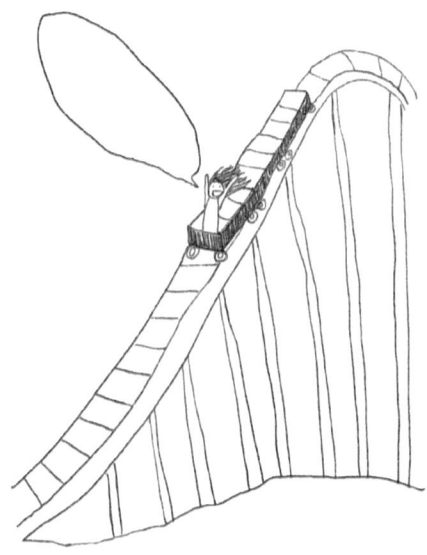

Where I Found You

I found you in the center of song,
where a patch of old sycamores grow.
There you hummed, a thick of harmonies,
in the key change of a tree, you sang.
And I plucked a fruit from your tune.
I thought I might take my leave then but
something marvelous was starting and
we needed to know what could be made
of us. So I crawled into your rests
and let my jazz free. As I wondered,

where do songs come from — where do they go?

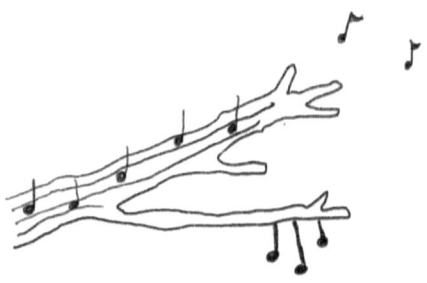

Late Afternoon

I dive to the bottom of the pool
          to catch the last of sun. Silver fish
                    on blue floors, a giant net of light–
                              I want to call something God here.

At the deep end, five gaping feet,
          I silhouette surrender
                    beneath the water's wide hold
                          & hold my finite breath.

But it's the furious impulse to come up for air
          that surprises me. A metal conviction
                    to survive, without a need for why–
                          is God inside my lungs?

When sky drops back to black goop
          my limbs shiver in the hindsight of light
                    and grow alive to my own
                    own existence

as I waggle my finger at objects in the house
          murmur about endings, call it all God
                    then give in, give in, to any small want
                    still here.

FALL

Fall is abstract, mystical, strange. The weather cools and the seasons change and somehow time gets warped in the shifting. Nostalgia steamrolls me, but the magic is strong. Revelations appear in parks, kitchens, backyards; everywhere there is something to notice. There is much to celebrate. So we do.

In The Fall

Something shushes summer
as September slants into a slumping fall.
Time all crinkled, trees crumpled,
a window cracked like a half-open eye,
I almost watch. As the past passes by
and waves its flagrant flags
and widens its wormhole mouth
and blows its gust of tunneling breath.
How did I get here, today?
How did I wake up one day in the next decade
while the past glitches on behind me,
parading its good time, behind me?
Even October looks back and moons me.
That glowing ass. Those trails of light
peeking through pale cracks. Trees turning
into burning bushes, prophesies
of what the gone will become.
Yesterday is dropping its edges,
spilling its wants into my now.
And I think I might be
living its dream soon-

Kid Magic

I once believed I was probably Matilda, that if I
stared at a pencil with the full thrust of my attention
and dared it to move half a half an inch,
it would. Or if I crept to the reptile house,
hissed Parseltongue to snakes,
tested *shhhs* for comprehension,
it'd work. There was never enough evidence
to prove otherwise. I could've always tried harder,
waited longer, done it a couple hundred more times,
and then, maybe then, who knows? After all,
how much can't be explained except by magic?
Who keeps the dried lavender upright and purple?
What causes two strangers to meet on a Sunday by the beach?
How do dogs find owners who need them,
how does anyone find anyone at all? I've aged but
my tendency for telekinesis is now just called manifesting,
my reptilian language now just a rhythm of words,
strange sayings slithering songlike into spells,
knocking on something invisible, something both out there
and here. Sometimes, when the words creak into each other
just right, or the heart quivers at some golden ratio,
a doorknob turns, and a world waits open.

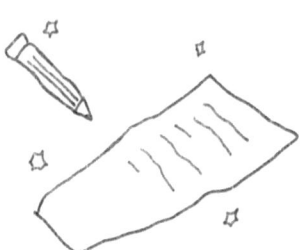

Bewitched

Another wonderless weeknight, I mutter.

I abracadabra the kitchen floor with a Swiffer,
  wishing for a whisk, a broomstick, an Oz.
    My roommate and I cackle and pop about our
      upset love potions, *Poisoned!* we snicker
        snapped & toiled & troubled but whatever,
          we drink it anyway, toast to the decadence
            of cake dinners on a Thursday. My gut rumbles,
              nostalgic for this very slice of time, & I am twistered

              into the storm of a bewildering thing—
              a flash-forward to me flashing back—

              and in the crystal ball eye of it all, I can see myself:
              a baby in one arm, a bottle of wine in the other,
                reliving that chapter with the Swiffer and the cake,
              when I had snapped up from a book & realized,
            with spellbinding clarity, that this is a damn good story,
          and I'm hungry & greedy to finish it,
        while whimper praying too, that it may never
      end, that I may never grow full

The Multiverse Hit Me Again

The multiverse hit me again today
at a paper goods store themed parrotfish
where another me sits behind the counter
doodling demons on a scrap.

I recognize the face of the wolf
our grandpa killed with a scythe.
Our dad used the tail as a broom, I tell her.
She draws my eyes on the head of a mop.

The fluorescent sky cracks, I am elsewhere
screaming up the trunk of a palm
about the linear project of misfortune.
I am in the middle of uncovering a secret

but my shape shifter time jumper resurrection
forgets the lesson again, again. I must hold tight
the slippery things I love. Root deep
the indubitable gut; the great okay.

Tomorrow, I'll tape up green cloth in every corner,
call it all grass and overgrown. Fancy myself Thumbelina,
tiny creature in a tulip. Plant longing in the pulp of a tree.
Understand myself as myth.

Not every version survives a wild beast,
I remind myself. I know what happens next.
I make myself a loose follower of time, pluck myself out
from the end of a prayer. Begin again, the millionth time.

In An Arena With Fear

I saw fear blush
from the unflappable stare
of my two ape-like eyes.
It was subtle, but enough.
So I made myself big
and beat my squishy chest
and sprung my body on
and ran and ran and ran
even as fear
took my throat and
rooted fingers taut and
cackled at the thrill of
fixing to an animal
so voraciously free.

To The Princess Of The Pea

"Nobody but a real princess
could be as sensitive as that."
–from The Princess and the Pea

princess
how did you come
to know the painful seat
of sensitivity

did you grow up a doll
plastic and pretty
forbidden to feel
any imperfect peace

or did you learn through thunder
how to keep close your soft center
and make yourself the eye
of weather and wrongs–

      did sensitivity
      become synonymous
      with the act of not giving up

so that of course you noticed
the tiny squish of a pea
twenty mattresses below
when the tender thing
gave in

Circling Clichés

I refuse originality, its heavy greed to be,
& shake the shaky hand, of fidgety clichés,
& step down from my point, and let my language free.

Yes I'll go over there, then come around and see,
Myself a spiral higher, yet still in that same place.[1]
Thus I refuse originality, its heavy greed to be.

I bless their grasses greener,
I bless my greening gray.
Away from all the pointing, I let my language free.

And on the grass: an apple, not far from its tree,
And around the tree a forest, a dense and glowing place.[2]
So I refuse originality, its heavy greed to be.

Live and let live, then follow that long lead,
And fall like silken water, a big and shifting shape.[3]
I step down from my point, and let my language free.

And somewhere within me, Light arches toward light.[4]
I refuse originality, its heavy greed to be,
And step down from my point, and let my language free.[5]

1. William Butler Yeats: "Life is a journey up a spiral staircase; as we grow older we cover the ground we have covered before, only higher up... The journey is both repetitive and progressive; we go both round and upward."

2. Robin Wall Kimmerer: "The trees act not as individuals, but somehow as a collective... what we see is the power of unity. What happens to one happens to us all. We can starve together or feast together."

3. Bruce Lee: "Be like water making its way through cracks... adjust to the object, and you shall find a way around or through it. If nothing within you stays rigid, outward things will disclose themselves... be formless, shapeless, like water."

4. Egyptian Book of the Dead (transl. Normandi Ellis): "I offer up life in return for life, pleasure for pleasure, light for light. It is good to rest in the fire."

5. Jessie Lian: In some circling, cyclical, cohesive & collaborative, light & liquid kind of way, we find the place we stand & the language we need.

Stills Of Time

1.

Drop of sunlight tucked inside time's flaky crunch:

I lick up what I can

2.

My clock has hung up its last breath, 6:45am:
a hefty squirrel now frozen mid-theft,
a chickadee's crow, echoing

through morning's luxurious sprawl.

I am watching.

for I have hungered for

stillness I have

3.

In a memory, I am rolling down a hill,

dirt   sky   dirt   sky

mud   blue   brown.

I am birthing the wind

falling & giving in
and it is pushing the world in
rotation dizzying myself in
laughter tickling the grass making love my
dirt sky dirt sky dirt my
looping time, collapsing in
to itself until it is just
a single place this
place

4.

Here you are. Holding on, even as sugar sifts through your
hands and scents slip past your nose, even as your fingers
dry up into dates

5.

Sunlight scoops up a toddler's hair,
kisses it invisible, a silver wing & a flame.
It is painless but we pray
that not everything would be taken.
Let us have another:
our squinty wants, our feathery wishes,
our golden golden afternoons

6.

I have glimpsed my future's face!
She is strange and ungainly,
unrecognizable,
chaotic glint & wild gait &
she has caught me in her hungry hook,
is reeling me in, her inevitable mouth, her
           inching   in   in   in

7.

Violet, amber, crimson and pink
                   carry the sun to its brink.
I follow, if only to lockstep my spin
          to the spin of the earth, glowing my hues,

be still, I still

                        as time also   stills

Heaven Now

I queen my body into summoning a breath.

An inhale of black sea, dark sky, skittish creature—
an inhale big banging inside of me.

Inside of me, evolution sprints toward its exhale.
A seed drifts on wind, a tired oak dies,

and the gates of heaven glow on the back
of some bewildered firefly flitting in my lung.

The afterlife flickers on and off. The past
and the future do a strange demon dance around me.

What can I do, but barefoot beat. But tiptoe twirl.
But melody my ocean sky, and spin and spin and spill.

I wait for the end. And watch it
get swallowed whole by another

beginning. Stardust, solidifying into atom.
I must wonder. Where is eternity, if not now?

Squeezed between two blinks, bottled inside a breath?

East Hollywood

I am inside a perpetual once upon a time
where every opening opens to another
and library books sneak out at full moon
crackle alive into neon flesh, polka-dotted bone
a stranger dressed in butterflies clutches my elbow
says with unbridled seriousness: *you're hottt*
and don't I feel it
as I cannonball into an exploding sky
my body electric with promise and plot
as a wild man on a wide piano sings about love
you gotta love it all while it lasts
and it lasts
tender tune tiptoeing back into belly
honey peach shrinking back into seed
mary's backyard caving back into lake
volcanic hot tub, thick eternal night
'til we scribble our selves back to story
become our own old mythical dream
breathless and vast, like stars in our lungs-
unfathomable. Forever is today and we
aren't missing anything.

Even After A Long While

I believe that these years of silence
stretching for ages between us
is only one long, drawn out,
beat —
a savory pause
in an ongoing conversation

And that brilliant pie of time
during which I had loved you
is still perfectly preserved
in the industrial freezer
that is my body
that is the infinite space
for terrible metaphors
and hilarious nonsensical
world widening home centering
friendship

That is, sometimes you meet someone
whose presence can't be undone
by time space death,
whose laughter squeal light
finds a way to steal into your bones
and live in you
and you can feel it waiting
waiting for that moment
when it will inevitably resurrect
and return to the body
from which it first came.

Dream Home

In my dream home,
the blankets will be made
out of a thick tomato soup,
and the pillows out of string quartets.
We'll bottle up campfires,
scrub them on like soap,
turn the backseats of our cars
into chairs for the kitchen table.

And in my dream home,
we'll live inside the quiet spaces
of words. The roof would be made
out of a capital *T*, refuge found
in the nook of an *e*. We'll lay atop
the canopy of an *r*, curl up
on a grassbed of commas and periods
beneath inky skies of apostrophes & quotes.

And in my dream home,
time will stand still
at half past the freckle
& a quarter to the hair
back when we had crossed our hearts and sworn
that we'd peter & pan for the rest of our lives,
never grow cynical, never lose hope,
never give up our childlike joy.

And in my dream home,
the walls will be made

out of coloring pages & notebook paper,
scribbled on by five-year-old hands,
handprints of high-fives pressed in
like concrete circling a groundbreaking.
There will be self-portraits of all of us,
us fearless, boneless, stick-figure giants,
arms made of tree branches
& fingers made of water hoses.
It meant we we would never run dry.

And in my dream home,
we'll see all our names
written in ink on the walls,
in our language, and our color,
and our favorite font *extra large,*
and if we were to say
any of the other strange names
written on the walls,
the owner of the name
would be willed into existence.
And we'd be companions for breakfast,
and sit together, and eat Cheerios,
fearlessly.

Nobody will tell you to go to your room when you cry
or to hide your face if it betrays your true emotion
or to cover up your messes whenever we have guests.

Because we'll tell you that
to be vulnerable is to have courage
to be weak is to invite love

to be low is to be high
to look up is to ground down.
We'll tell you all sorts of apparent paradoxes
and we'll swear by them each morning
until we realize their truths.

And in my dream home,
the words we had hoped for
will finally be made flesh,
the stories of hope
transformed into nonfiction.

And this is how we will grow up.
Further up, and further in.

Communion

1.

We pass the smoke around the fire,
We breathe in the same good earth.
Go ahead, speak your anxiety free,
Or take a seat, in the field of your quiet.
The embers will prick the dark like stars,
They'll offer you sweet constellations.
Make yourself a big dipper, make yourself a wish,
Then rock the twinkling night 'til it's swaddled up in sleep.
Sleep. It will be here when you wake
Though the you that you knew
Will be replaced by someone new,
Someone a little freer,
Someone a little more true.

2.

I woke up in the lap of some
Daily miracle, which whispered
In my ear about how everything,
Everything, pulses with life
Like an invitation inhaling us
Into the world's giant heart.
The miracle is this:
You belong here.
You dance the waters fall,
You laugh the hillsides full,
You breathe the oceans flow,
You free the oak tree grow.
The sky fruits, the tree balloons,
The river storms, the air shapes,
While you invite the earth and everything,
Everything, into your giant heart.

Acknowledgements

Thank you to the editors of these publications, where these poems were first published: Curio Cabinet Magazine: "Breadcrumbs"; Hot Pot Magazine: "How To Make Dumplings"; Star82 Review: "Wintering Sun," "The Faucet Is Leaking"; The Los Angeles Press: "Heaven Now," "Excessive Heat Warning"; Wildroof Journal: "Love, A Shapeshifter"

This book would not be in existence without every single word of encouragement that has come my way. Thank you–

To Emma Murf for editing my poems, watching me cry, and being perhaps the greatest force behind why this book was birthed.

To the Pezestrians Poetry Group for pouring your insight & laughter into my work. My poems are alive because of you.

To all the open mics that gave me space & inspired me big & made me feel like I had a voice with weight & worth.

To Melissa Zhu, Leah Kelley, and Makario Lewis, for believing in me from the very beginning, until I could believe in myself too. I kept going because of you.

To Steven Gizzi for your thoughtful & loving attention toward my work & my being. You are my rock.

To mom & dad & brother for your unconditional love, and for

showing me how to walk through the world with curiosity and wonder.

To every single person who has ever dunked me in affirmation. I take your words with me everywhere I go.

And to you, dear reader! For choosing to spend time with me here in this big wide world.

ABOUT THE AUTHOR

Jessie Lian is a tender being seeking big feelings in small moments. Her writing practice began in her 3rd grade diary, and her love of musicality from memorizing her dad's favorite Chinese poems based on sound instead of meaning. It was the enthusiasm of an audience at a church open mic that then propelled her to take her poetry more seriously. She continued to find catharsis at open mics around Atlanta while sneaking poems into Excel sheets at her corporate job. And in the vast space of the pandemic, she started a weekly poetry workshop with a friend; this was the group that marked a turning point for her craft. She is a now someone who is very proud of herself for publishing her first book.

www.ingramcontent.com/pod-product-compliance
Lightning Source LLC
Chambersburg PA
CBHW030504130626
46549CB00007B/2844